What Is Truth?

The Best of the
CHRISTIAN RESEARCH
JOURNAL

ISBN 978-0-9819587-5-0

CONTENTS

INTRODUCTION

I t is not too much to say that truth is under siege in the postmodern world. As such, those who see truth as relative, subjective, or pragmatic are seen as tolerant and enlightened. Conversely, those who see truth as objectively rooted and grounded in the person and work of Jesus Christ are considered intolerant or even arrogant.

Perhaps no one embodies the spirit of our age better than our newly elected president. While biblical orthodoxy defines sin as *being out of alignment with God's standard of perfection*, Barack Obama defines sin as *"being out of alignment with my values."*[1] A more consequential—and frightening—example of postmodern relativism is difficult to imagine.

First, if sin is being out of alignment with President Obama's values, then Mr. Obama, rather than the Almighty, becomes the arbiter of right and wrong. Furthermore, if sin is being out of alignment with one's own system of values, the United States of America is hardly justified in passing judgment on Osama Bin Laden. Why? Because Osama sees great value in atrocities such as the Manhattan Massacre. Finally, if sin is being out of alignment with one's own personal values, then truth is a mere matter of preference or opinion.

As an organization, the Christian Research Institute has the *spiritual* resources necessary to prevail in a battle for truth. Indeed, for years the CHRISTIAN RESEARCH JOURNAL has been on the cutting edge of this battle. That's why we've now bundled the best articles on truth, tolerance, and postmodernism from the JOURNAL and re-present them here in this handsome hardcover edition to equip you to stand in the battle. Because truth is under siege, your prayers and finances are more crucial than ever before. Without you those resources would never reach the frontlines. That is why I am so grateful for your partnership in ministry. Your gifts empowered by prayer are playing a strategic role in the battle for truth.

Hank Hanegraaff
Charlotte, North Carolina

---

1. Cathleen Falsani, "Barack Obama: The 2004 'God Factor' Interview Transcript," http://falsani.blogspot.com/2008/04/barack-obama-2004-god-factor-interview.html, accessed March 30, 2009.

ASK HANK

What Is Truth?

"'You are a king, then!' said Pilate. Jesus answered, 'You are right in saying I am a king. In fact, for this reason I was born, and for this I came into the world, to testify to the truth. Everyone on the side of truth listens to me.' 'What is truth?' Pilate asked." —John 18:37-38

This is the very question Pontius Pilate asked Jesus. In the irony of the ages, he stood toe-to-toe with the embodiment of truth and yet missed its reality. Postmodern people are in much the same position. They stare at truth but fail to recognize its identity.

First, truth is an aspect of the nature of God himself. Thus, to put on truth is to put on Christ. For Christ is "truth" (John 14:6), and Christians are to be the bearers of truth. As Os Guinness explains, Christianity is not true because it works (pragmatism); it is not true because it feels right (subjectivism); it is not true because it is "my truth" (relativism). It is true because it is anchored in the person of Christ.

Furthermore, truth is anything that corresponds to reality. As such, truth does not yield to the size and strength of the latest lobby group. Nor is truth merely a matter of preference or opinion. Rather truth is true even if everyone denies it, and a lie is a lie even if everyone affirms it.

Finally, truth is essential to a realistic world view. When sophistry, sensationalism, and superstition sabotage truth, our view of reality is seriously skewed. The death of truth spells the death of civilization. However, as Aleksandr Solzhenitsyn discovered, "One word of truth outweighs the entire world."—*Hank Hanegraaff*

For Further Study, See Os Guinness, *Time for Truth* (Grand Rapids: Baker Books, 2000).

Hank Hanegraaff is author of several award-winning, bestselling books, including *Christianity in Crisis*, *Counterfeit Revival*, *Resurrection*, and *The Prayer of Jesus*. He is president of the Christian Research Institute and host of the *Bible Answer Man* broadcast.

Originally published in Hank Hanegraaff, *The Bible Answer Book* (Nashville: J. Countryman, 2004).

THE POSTMODERN CHALLENGE

Facing the Spirit of the Age

by Jim Leffel and Dennis McCallum

W e live in strange times. Until recently, Christianity was under fire at most universities because it was thought to be unscientific, and consequently, untrue. Today, Christianity is widely rejected merely because it claims to be true! Increasingly, academics regard anyone claiming to know any objective or universal truth as intolerant and arrogant.

THE NEW SPIRITUAL CONSENSUS

What accounts for this bizarre and growing consensus? It's called *postmodernism*. According to certain enormously influential thinkers, truth is essentially political. Truth claims are created by "belief communities," not *discovered* by reason, observation, or revelation. Lynne Cheney, former chairperson of the National Endowment for the Humanities, recently reported to Congress that the academic community is experiencing a major ideological shift toward postmodernism.[1]

Postmodernism is more than a movement among intellectuals. It deeply affects the broader culture.[2] In fact, academic postmod-

SYNOPSIS

"Openness" (without the restraint of reason) and "tolerance" that rejects all moral absolutes are the mandates of postmodern ideology. This thinking has dominated America's "politically correct" universities for over a decade. Moreover, postmodernism is gaining a clear and growing consensus in popular culture. Consequently, Christians today face unique challenges as we seek to communicate the gospel in a compelling way. In order to speak to the "it's true for me because I believe it" mentality, Christian communicators must understand and critique the foundations of postmodern relativism. We must also develop new and creative pre-evangelistic approaches to establish common ground with our secular culture.

ernism has galvanized the latent relativism growing in American culture since the 60s, while giving it a respectability it never had before. The new postmodern outlook is now everybody's business. George Barna shows that over 80 percent of Americans today are basically relativistic, and the evangelical church is not far behind.[3] Meanwhile, the church in North America is not answering postmodernists effectively, and we are losing ground so rapidly that many church leaders are ready to join the new postmodern consensus.

We must understand the thinking behind this growing consensus if we are to communicate effectively with our culture. We also need to understand it in order to protect our families and churches. In this article, we explain what postmodernism is and how it has affected people's religious views. Then we offer a strategy for reaching postmodern thinkers.

ARROGANCE AND RELIGIOUS TRUTH

Not long ago, "Dear Abby" commented on religious disagreements. She printed a letter from one of her critics: "Your answer to the woman who complained that her relatives were always arguing with her about religion was ridiculous. You advised her to simply declare the subject off-limits. Are you suggesting that people talk about only trivial, meaningless subjects so as to avoid a potential controversy?... It is arrogant to tell people there are subjects they may not mention in your presence. You could have suggested she learn enough about her relatives' cult to show them the errors contained in its teaching." Abby replied, "In my view, the height of arrogance is to attempt to show people the 'errors' in the religion of their choice."[4]

Abby's postmodern response typifies today's popular thinking about religious tolerance and faith commitments. Notice two key ideas implied in her comment. First, challenging another's religious truth claims is arrogant. Second, *personal choice* alone legitimizes spiritual commitments.

Why do so many today consider it arrogant to suggest that someone's religious beliefs might be wrong? By arrogant, most people mean intolerant — a term that has come to have a whole new meaning in recent years. Intolerance used to refer to bigotry or prejudice — that is, attacking people or excluding them because of who they are or what they think. In that sense, intolerance is offensive. But now, intolerance often means simply asserting some beliefs are true and others are false.

The recent movie *At Play in the Fields of the Lord* illustrates this point. In a conversation between an Amazonian Indian and a Christian missionary, the Indian says, "If the Lord made Indians the way they are, who are you people to make them different?" This is one of the defining sentiments of our day. Attempting to convert people is unacceptable because it implies standing in judgment over their "truth."

CAN TRUTH BE OBJECTIVE?

At the heart of the issue is whether or not objective truth exists. Objective truth means truth that is independent of individual or cultural belief. When something is objectively true (like the existence of the moon), it's true for everyone regardless of whether they acknowledge it or not. Objectivity assumes we all live in one reality, even though we may experience it differently or have different beliefs about it. Those of us who believe in objective truth think that we have a common base from which to discuss what is true and what isn't, because we all live in the same real world.

Postmodernists deny this shared reality. Instead, they claim that different cultural groups live in different realities. To them, a people's reality is their *perception* or *interpretation* of the external world, and is not the world itself. Postmodernists claim we are really creating truth as we interpret. We are not discovering truth. According to postmodernists, a thing is true because I believe it, I do not believe it because it is true.[5]

As Christians, we accept the reality of both *subjective* and *objective* truth, and we believe we can discover both through a combination of our own reason and revelation. The Bible teaches we can come to know a love that transcends knowledge (Eph. 3:19), and that relationship with God goes beyond mere statements of fact about God. This is subjective or experiential truth. But the reality of subjective or experiential truth in no way rules out the reality of objective truth. Postmodernists, on the other hand, think all truth is subjective. On this, we can never agree.

The Bible's emphasis on historical revelation (1 Cor. 15:13-15), doctrinal propositions (Rom. 10:9), and natural revelation (1:18-20) presume that objective truth exists. This places Christians in direct opposition to postmodern thinking.

POSTMODERNISM MEANS THE DEATH OF TRUTH

Today, higher education openly promotes cynicism about truth and reason.[6] Educators argue that every time people claim to be in possession of the truth (especially religious truth), they end up repressing those who don't agree. Today, it's more stylish to make no truth claims at all. How has this surprising outlook gained such wide acceptance in history's most advanced civilization? To understand this, we need to look at how postmodernists conceive the past three hundred years of Western history.

Postmodernism abandons *modernism*, the humanist philosophy of the European Enlightenment. Enlightenment thinking began with French philosopher Rene Descartes's idea of the *autonomous man* — the one who starts from his own thought ("I think, therefore I am"). Beginning from himself, and explicitly excluding any need for God or revelation, Enlightenment man systematically builds his world view from reason alone.

Modernists assumed the mind is a "mirror of nature," meaning that our perceptions of reality actually correspond to the way the world is. From this presumption, modernists pursued their vision of *progress,* exalting technological achievement and mastery over nature. Expansion-minded capitalism, liberal democracy, and communism — all outgrowths of modernist thought — have sought to subjugate the earth to the Eurocentric outlook.

Modernism, however, planted the seeds of its own undoing. As modernists have conquered the globe in the name of progress, those they oppressed and marginalized have increasingly asked, "Progress toward what?" Postmodernists say modern rationalism and technological proliferation have brought us to the brink of disaster. The myth of "modern progress" ends up in a nightmare of violence, both for the people it marginalizes and for the earth itself. That's why so many people today are interested in primal cultures and world views that promote the unity of humanity with nature, rather than humankind standing over nature.

Postmodernists offer some good critiques of humanism, progress, and autonomous reason. More importantly, Enlightenment rationalists have never demonstrated that human reason can arrive at ultimate truths without divine revelation. As Christians, we have never accepted the modernist claim that technological advancement and human reason will solve all social problems.

Atheistic existentialist writers such as Nietzsche and Sartre prepared the way for contemporary postmodernism. They realized the modernist rejection of the transcendent was a costly proposition because it annihilated all standards of objective morality, human value, and truth.[7] Viewed in this way, postmodernism is the logical extension of modernist thought: it exposes autonomous human reason as a dead end.

While Christians should welcome much of postmodernism's critique of modernism, we see that their critique is based on equally dubious assumptions and will lead to disastrous conclusions. The rhetorical power of postmodern terms like "tolerance," "openness," and "inclusion" effectively disguises a more insidious objective — the destruction of all absolute truth claims. Postmodern openness to spirituality may seem like a positive step away from modernist naturalism, but this kind of spirituality is inherently anti-Christian because it considers the Christian message (like all world views) true only for those who accept it as such.[8]

POSTMODERN ANTIHUMANISM

Rather than see humans as individual rational selves, as modernists held, postmodernists think of humans as extensions of culture. They deny the individual self altogether. Postmodern psychologist and social critic Kenneth Gergen says, "With the spread of postmodern consciousness, we see the demise of personal definition, reason, authority. . . . All intrinsic properties of the human being, along with moral worth and personal commitment, are lost from view."[9]

Postmodern anthropology is based on the idea that humans are "social constructs" or socially determined beings. Our outlooks and perceptions are all the result of our enculturation. Peter Berger explains what is called sociology of *knowledge* — the idea that all knowledge is the product of our culture and language:

A thought of any kind is grounded in society . . . The individual, then, derives his worldview socially in very much the same way that he derives his roles and his identity. In other words, his emotions and his self-interpretation like his actions are predefined for him by society, and so is his cognitive approach to the universe that surrounds him.[10]

Rather than conceiving the mind as a mirror of nature, postmodernists argue that we bend nature through the lens of culture and language.[11] This leads them to reject the possibility of discovering objective truth since each culture approaches reality differently, depending on its language, its particular needs, and its historical conditions. To know objectively we would have to transcend our cultural lens, and according to postmodernists, this is impossible.

In place of objective truth and what postmodernists call "metanarratives" (comprehensive world views), postmodernists point to "local narratives," or stories about reality that "work" for particular communities, but have no validity beyond that community. Indeed, postmodernists reject the whole language of truth and reality in favor of literary terms like *narrative* and *story*.[12] So-called reality is all about interpretation, not about what's true.[13]

Postmodernists hold that when modernists or religionists advance objective truth, they do violence by excluding other voices; that is, they regard other world views to be invalid. Thus the ideas of truth and reason marginalize the vulnerable by "scripting them out of the story." Truth claims, we are told, are merely tools to legitimize power. Michel Foucault writes, "We cannot exercise power except through the production of truth."[14] For postmodernists, truth claims are really mere propaganda intended to dismiss other views by calling them superstition or nonsense. That's why, in postmodern culture, the person to be feared is the one who believes he or she knows ultimate truth. The *dogmatist*, the *totalizer*, the *absolutist* is both naive and dangerous, not to mention arrogant.

Rather than dominating others with our "version of reality," postmodernists call us to accept all beliefs as equally valid. Instead of one truth, we have many truths. Openness without the restraint of reason along with tolerance without moral appraisal are the new postmodern mandates.

PERSONAL BELIEFS DEFINE TRUTH

In postmodern culture, it's impossible to separate what people believe from who they are, because the act of believing something makes it true (for those who believe). Therefore, rejecting the *content* of faith means rejecting the *person* who constructed that truth. Truth now means personal preference and personal empowerment. It would be no more appropriate to question the validity of a person's belief than to critique his or her choice from a dinner menu. Striving together to discover truth through debate and spirited discussion is definitely out.

Consider current opinion about the religions of the world. Few people understand much about them. Yet most people believe they all teach pretty much the same thing. The real concern is finding spirituality that "fits." George Barna's research shows that "about four out of every ten adults strongly concurred that when Christians, Jews, Buddhists, and others pray to their god, all of those individuals are actually praying to the same god, but simply use different names for that deity. Only one out of every six adults strongly disagreed with this view." [15]

America today is a religious smorgasbord. The only question seems to be, " For what are you hungry?" And taste is more important than substance. That's why people are largely unmoved if we point out that their beliefs are hopelessly contradictory or irrational.

Most people "absorb" this postmodern outlook rather than think their way into it. An impressive majority of Americans believe that truth is relative.[16] Few, however, know why they think that way. Still fewer have any clue about how their beliefs relate to their own lives in a practical way. In general, people are more ideologically confused than they are deeply committed to their convictions. As a result, while we hear the rhetoric of openness to everything and tolerance for everyone, we rarely find anyone who really understands what this means. Relativism is just the socially appropriate attitude of the hour. Postmodern ideologues have successfully transformed ideology into popular zeitgeist.

Ironically, in an age of antidogmatism, this radical subjectivity leads to the dangerously arrogant inference that people can never be wrong about what they believe. If we are free from the constraints of rationality, nothing separates truth from self-delusion. Gergen's words are both candid and chilling: "Evaluation can only take place from within a perspective. . . . If in my view 'objective truth' is a misleading term, I can scarcely condemn a theory because it is objectively false."[17]

The age of antidogmatism ends up being the age of anti-intellectualism. Truth has been replaced, especially among many academics, by politically empowering narrative.[18] This kind of thinking is the foundation of revisionist history,[19] feminist critical method,[20] and many of the current formulations of multiculturalism.[21]

In the postmodern climate of openness and tolerance, beliefs become barriers against genuine dialogue about spiritual and moral truth. For example, political correctness advocates, such as Stanley Fish, have argued that since all speech is a political power play, ideas must be monitored and managed, not rationally and constructively engaged.[22] Such controlling attitudes lead even liberal academics like Harvard's Alan Dershowitz to claim that a new McCarthyism pervades intellectual life today.[23]

History offers a warning that such antirational dogmatism can exact a high price. Indeed, a daunting historical and philosophical link exists between postmodern "constructivism" and fascism. Both reject objective truth; both assert that there is no essential human nature or inherent human rights; both celebrate the substitution of power for truth. Interestingly, major contributors to the development of postmodern ideology, such as Martin Heidegger and Paul de Mann, were deeply committed fascists.[24]

Postmodern subjectivism also inhibits a deep commitment to

one's own beliefs. Since faith is rooted in the practical matters of personal taste and experience, people tend to adopt and abandon beliefs according to the demands of the moment. After all, when truth is a human creation rather than something independent of ourselves, we may casually move on to some new "truth" whenever it suits us. How tragic it is when friends tell us, "I tried Christianity for a while, but it just didn't work for me."

CROSSCULTURAL COMMUNICATION

Today evangelical Christians stand at a greater distance from those with whom we communicate than we did just 20 years ago. At that time, even those who rejected Christianity were prepared to discuss whether the evidence for Christianity's truth was adequate. Today, this is much less frequently the case. Before we can broach the question of whether the Christian gospel is true, we have to establish that such a thing as truth exists.

To bridge the gap between ourselves and postmodern thinkers, we need to introduce additional steps in the communication process. Communicating with postmodern culture is not *impossible*; it's just *more difficult*.

Suppose a villager in another land engaged you in a conversation about how to fend off the forest worm-demons, who are boring holes in people's teeth. At some point, you would probably interrupt that villager. "Excuse me," you would say with your hand raised. "We have a problem here. I can't share my views about how to fend off these demons because I don't believe they exist!"

The gap between the villager's starting point and your starting point is too great for you to discuss demon countermeasures. This is why success in crosscultural communication requires more patience and care in approaching each discussion. Crosscultural missionaries may spend years learning the language and culture of those to whom they minister. Meanwhile, careless communicators are rarely successful in a crosscultural context, and they menace the ministry of other Christians as they blithely offend people in the name of Christ. Similarly, if we are to be successful communicators with postmodern people, including our own children and their friends, we will have to understand the postmodern outlook.

THE ANTIRATIONAL REACTION

We don't agree with some evangelical leaders who have suggested that truth-oriented or rational witnessing won't work in the postmodern era. It has to work. If we argue that a truth-oriented gospel won't win people today, we are really arguing that people can't be won at all. Whatever "gospel" to which we win people without truth is certainly not the Christian gospel. Our message is unique, not because it leads to the most far-out spiritual experience, but because it is true. Paul ministered in a comparably nonrationalistic culture, but he didn't hesitate to "persuade" people (2 Cor. 5:11. See also Acts 17:2-4).

We dare not join the rush to dispense with reason and so-called "left-brain" arguments. The day we dispense with reason is the same day we dispense with truth. After all, if one proposition can be true, and its opposite is also true, what is a lie? God's truth doesn't depend on our thoughts. It is true regardless of what we think. But this sort of truth, objective truth, cannot exist apart from rational categories.

Of course, we are not suggesting that Christians merely offer objective truth while witnessing. We believe that relationship is more important than ever in a postmodern world. Demonstrating Christian love, Christlike lives, and experiencing the power of God are extremely important today, but these should supplement and illustrate the truth of the gospel, not replace it.

THAWING OUT POSTMODERN DOGMATISM

At Xenos Fellowship, we too have been struggling with the riddle of dialogue with postmodern culture. We have had some success and can suggest some promising directions for Christians to explore.

First, we find that Socratic or dialogue-based pre-evangelism is good for undermining the formulas that paralyze people's minds and prevent them from comprehending God's truth. Dialogue — specifically raising questions — is more palatable to postmodern hearers than authoritative declarations. Later, when they are more able to hear and think, we need to call them to moral and intellectual accountability to God. But again, we need extra steps before we reach that point.

Next, we need a strategy intended to move postmodern thinkers to the point where traditional pleas and arguments will finally take effect. We use questions (1) to discover and understand people's presuppositions, and clarify those presuppositions in their own minds; (2) to move our hearers carefully to the point of tension created by the internal contradictions inherent in the postmodern outlook; and (3) to help them realize the problems with their existing view, thus creating a new receptiveness. Then comes the time to supply the Christian alternative.

DISCOVERING PRESUPPOSITIONS

When talking to members of postmodern culture, we find that few fully comprehend the bases for their views. Therefore, we aim to help them understand their own views, along with some of the problems inherent in those views.

We like to gather groups of Christians together with their non-Christian friends in a home for a "Conversation and Cuisine event" (dinner party-discussion group). We assure guests in advance that all views are welcome, and that this is not a church meeting, where they have to give a "right" answer. After dinner, the discussion topic might be, "To Judge or Not to Judge." The discussion facilitator presents situations involving different types of judgments, and the group discusses whether they would feel comfortable making a judgment in those situations.

---

1. Your white workmate is helping an African-American workmate to unravel a problem in the computer database. You overhear the white worker in his frustration call the African American a dumb N___. She looks up with hurt on her face. You denounce the white worker for being prejudiced and for hurting her feelings.

---

2. Your other friend at work announces she is getting divorced. She has fallen in love with another man, and although she has two children, she has told her husband she cannot continue to live a lie. Her husband and children are crushed, but she feels she must be true to herself. You charge her with selfishness, lack of loyalty, and willingness to hurt others' feelings.

For example: Most postmodern-influenced thinkers will be more willing to approve passing judgment in scenario no. 1 than in scenario no. 2. Why? Both judgments involve someone hurting the feelings of another. While people might raise several valid points (such as the fact that we don't know what the adulterer's husband was like), the main effect of the pairing is to create confusion.

At this point, the facilitator raises an interesting question: "How would people have answered these same questions 30 years ago?" Most agree that people would have made the judgment on the bottom (no. 2) without hesitation two or three decades ago. At the same time, though people might have resented the racial epithet on the left (no. 1) 30 years ago, they may have concluded that "sticks and stones will break my bones, but names will never hurt me." Today, most secular people believe that the crime in no. 1 is morally far worse than that in no. 2, if indeed no. 2 represents anything wrong at all — just the reverse of what the same crowd would have concluded 30 years before.

Why the difference between today and 30 years ago? Postmodern thinkers invariably respond that judgments have changed because morality is not objective, but a product of cultural paradigms. Now we pose a very important question: So are we suggesting that using the "N" word was o.k. 30 years ago? Or was it wrong, but they just *thought* it was o.k.?

This question causes postmodern thinkers to be confused. If they say it was really all right to call someone by this name at one time, they are condoning the racism of the past. But if they say people only thought it was all right, they are suggesting that a universal standard of right and wrong exists. Either position contradicts central postmodern assumptions.

By struggling with these internal contradictions in an accepting atmosphere, postmodern-influenced people realize they are willing to judge, but their own unspoken rules governing judgment perplex them. Modernists — those who are agnostic or atheistic and who trust rationality — have problems here as well. They have no more solid basis for moral judgments than postmodernists, and neither can they explain why they hold to moral views now or in the past. Underlying the whole question is the obvious need for moral authority.

MOVING HEARERS INTO TENSION

Of course, we don't want to merely leave people confused. We create confusion in order to break down the dogmatism of postmodern thinking. When we can't answer questions about our own view, it suggests that our ready-made formulas are inadequate, and something more is needed.

The same group discussing judgment later introduces another scenario:

3. You visit an African tribe during their female circumcision ritual and behold a teenage girl receiving a clitorectomy. When you complain to your tour guide, he points out your Eurocentric values are interfering with your judgment.

This scenario raises more complicated contradictions for the postmodern thinker. Female circumcision is a manifestation of misogyny and male control over women. The procedure guarantees that women will never experience orgasm, and, therefore, will take no pleasure from sex. In the words of one African apologist, the practice "frees women from their bondage to lust to find their true identity as mothers." The girls have little or no say in whether they receive the procedure. Viewed objectively, this practice is a savage and brutal violation of women and should be especially abhorrent to feminists.

But there's a problem! Female circumcision is also a time-honored religious rite of passage in *another culture*, and an oppressed, nonwestern, nonwhite culture at that. It is, therefore, off-limits to postmodern judgment of any kind. In culturally postmodern groups, we will often find those who agree with the tour guide. They feel we cannot judge this situation because we have no context from which to view it other than our own cultural "reality." Meanwhile, this dilemma confuses other postmodern-influenced thinkers. Condoning female genital mutilation naturally makes the women in the group nervous.

But that's not all. Suppose we consider New Guinea, where for centuries tribes have hunted members of other tribes and taken their heads as fetishes. Today, under the influence of Western colonial culture, the government of New Guinea has outlawed head-hunting. Do those in our discussion group agree with this move or not? More confusion. The militant postmodernists stand their ground. "How can we judge a practice that's been going on for hundreds of years, and is a religious practice to boot?" "Who do we think we are to judge this culture, when we have x, y, and z evils in our own culture?"

Their point seems credible even though they are condoning murder. They are merely repeating a truth Francis Schaeffer observed two decades ago: "If there is no absolute by which to judge the state [or here, the culture] then the state [culture] is absolute."[25] We have to agree that for us to judge events in another culture isn't possible apart from the existence of a moral absolute that applies to all cultures, whether they know it or not. When we put such a point on it, the postmodernists' position either hardens or crumbles.[26]

When hard-line postmodern thinkers defend murder, others in the room often groan in discomfort. We might not win the most militant postmodernists, but remember that the majority of our culture follows postmodern ideals as they do clothing fashions. They are not deeply committed to the postmodern agenda, and if they find these assumptions failing the test in situations like this one, they will reconsider.

TIMING IN COMMUNICATION

We don't share the gospel itself at these discussions. The Conversation and Cuisine events are pre-evangelistic. If the guests from that discussion go home rethinking their positions, our pre-evangelistic task is complete and successful for the time being. We have moved them beyond the point where formulas like, "That's nice for you" have insulated them from engagement in real discussion.

Hopefully, we are in relationship with these people and can follow up on our first conversations with them. Once their minds are less bound, and, provided we also strengthen the message with subjective, relational witness, we should eventually succeed in sharing the gospel as objective truth.

POSTMODERN OPPORTUNITIES

If we learn the rules in today's society, we may find new opportunities for successful witness that hadn't been present in earlier, modernist culture. After all, the New Testament church grew in a world similar to our postmodern view. Also, the most vigorous parts of the body of Christ today come from Asia, Africa, and Latin America. Christianity is increasingly hard to characterize as "Western." Most important, the nihilism and loneliness of postmodern culture cry out for the love of God in millions of aching hearts. If we love others, rely on God's power, and stay faithful to the truth, we will see many come to know Him.

Jim Leffel is elder of Xenos Christian Fellowship and director of the Crossroads Project, an apologetics ministry in Columbus, Ohio. **Dennis McCallum** is Lead Pastor at Xenos Christian Fellowship, also in Columbus, and author of several books. They are coauthors of *The Death of Truth* (Bethany House), which assesses the advance of the postmodern outlook in society today.

This article originally appeared in *Christian Research Journal*, volume 19, number 2 (1996).

---

1 See Lynne V. Cheney, "Telling the Truth: A Report on the State of the Humanities in Higher Education" (Washington, DC: National Endowment for the Humanities, September 1992).
2 See our book, Jim Leffel and Dennis McCallum, *The Death of Truth* (Minneapolis: Bethany House Publishers, 1996), for an explanation of how postmodernism encroaches on every important aspect of contemporary culture.
3 George Barna shows that postmodern thinking in secular culture is thriving in the evangelical church. See George Barna, *What Americans Believe: An Annual Survey of Values and Religious Views in the United States* (Ventura, CA: Regal Books, 1991).
4 "Deciding whether to Discuss Religion Prompts Debate," in "Dear Abby," 19 September 1989.

5 See a clear explanation of this view in Richard Rorty, *Contingency, Irony, and Solidarity* (Cambridge: Cambridge University Press, 1989), xiii-10.

6 Cheney, 7.

7 Friedrich Nietzsche, "The Gay Science," in Walter Kaufmann, *The Portable Nietzsche* (New York: Viking Press, 1954), 93-102; Jean-Paul Sartre, *Essays in Existentialism* (Secaucus, NJ: The Citadel Press, 1965), 31-62.

8 We are concerned that the growing number of evangelical scholars attracted to postmodernism have not dealt sufficiently with this point. An example is J. Richard Middleton and Brian Walsh, *Reality Isn't What It Used to Be* (Downers Grove, IL: InterVarsity Press, 1994), 88-171.

9 Kenneth Gergen, *The Saturated Self* (New York: Basic Books, 1991), 22829.

10 Peter Berger, *Invitation to Sociology* (Garden City, NJ: Doubleday & Co., 1963), 117. Berger would not call himself a postmodernist, but his ideas have been extremely influential in postmodern circles.

11 A defining work detailing this position is Frederick Jameson, *The Prison House of Language* (Princeton: Princeton University Press, 1972).

12 Jacques Derrida, "Structure, Sign and Play in the Discourse of the Human Sciences," in *Writing and Difference,* trans. Alan Bass (Chicago: University of Chicago Press, 1978), 278-93.

13 For an excellent discussion of this point, see Roger Lundin, *Culture of Interpretation* (Grand Rapids: Eerdmans, 1993).

14 Michel Foucault, *Power/Knowledge* (New York: Pantheon Books, 1980), 132.

15 Barna, 275.

16 Ibid., 83-85.

17 Gergen, 229.

18 See, e.g., Paula S. Rothenber, *Racism and Sexism: An Integrated Study* (New York: St. Martins Press, 1988), 6-7, 350.

19 See, e.g., Ellen Somekawa and Elizabeth A. Smith, "Theorizing the Writing of History or, I Can't Think Why It Should Be So Dull, For a Great Deal of It Must Be Invention," *Journal of Social History,* Fall 1988, 154.

20 See, e.g., Margaret A. Farley, "Feminist Consciousness and the Interpretation of Scripture," in Letty M. Russell, ed., *Feminist Interpretation of the Bible* (Philadelphia: The Westminster Press, 1985).

21 See, e.g., Christine E. Sleeter, ed., *Empowerment through Multicultural Education* (Albany: State of New York Press, 1991).

22 Stanley Fish, "There's No Such Thing as Free Speech and It's a Good Thing Too," *Boston Review,* February 1992, 3.

23 Alan M. Dershowitz, "Harvard Witch Hunt Burns the Incorrect at the

Stake," *Los Angeles Times*, Washington ed., 22 April 1992, A11.

24 For an excellent introduction to these comparisons, see Gene Edward Veith, *Modern Fascism* (St. Louis: Concordia Publishing House, 1993).

25 Francis Schaeffer, *How Shall We Then Live?* (film series), episode 10.

26 See several other examples of Conversation and Cuisine discussions as well as other articles on postmodernism at the Crossroads Project website: http://www.xenos.org/ministries/crossroads/.

DECONSRUCTING LIBERAL TOLERANCE

by Francis J. Beckwith

Our assessments of the future are always at the mercy of un-expected contingencies. Perhaps, like the Berlin Wall, cur-rent academic and cultural fads that challenge Christian orthodoxy will soon crumble by the sheer force of their internal con-tradictions, coupled by the ascendancy of both the vibrant movement of Christian thinkers within the discipline of philosophy and the growing criticism of Darwinism and naturalism by Phillip Johnson and others. Perhaps. But barring such a near-miraculous cultural turnaround, I offer a number of observations. This article will suggest

SYNOPSIS

Liberal Tolerance is perhaps the primary challenge to the Christian worldview current in North American popular culture. Proponents of this viewpoint argue that it is intolerant and inconsistent with the principles of a free and open society for Christians (and others) to claim that their moral and religious perspective is correct and ought to be embraced by all citizens. Liberal tolerance is not what it appears to be, however. It is a partisan philosophical perspective with its own set of dogmas. It assumes, for instance, a relativistic view of moral and religious knowledge. This assumption has shaped the way many people think about issues such as homosexuality, abortion rights, and religious truth claims, leading them to believe that a liberally tolerant posture concerning these issues is the correct one and that it ought to be reflected in our laws and customs. But this posture is dogmatic, intolerant, and coercive, for it asserts that there is only one correct view on these issues, and if one does not comply with it, one will face public ridicule, demagogic tactics, and perhaps legal reprisals. Liberal Tolerance is neither liberal nor tolerant.

some ways that Christian thinkers and cultural critics may defend their faith if present trends continue.

First, do you remember the words of John Lennon, put to song in the mid-1970s?

Imagine there's no heaven; It's easy if you try
No hell below us; Above us only sky....
Imagine no possessions; It isn't hard to do
Nothing to kill or die for; And no religion too
You may say I'm a dreamer, but I'm not the only one
Someday you'll join us, and the world will be as one.

Those who came of age under the tutelage of Lennon and his contemporaries are now dominant in our most prestigious institutions of cultural influence: law, education, the media, and the social sciences. Although the optimism of these former flower children may be waning, their totalitarian impulses, implied in Lennon's call for global unanimity on matters controversial, are in full bloom. We will call their project *liberal tolerance*.

RELATIVISM: THE GROUND OF
LIBERAL TOLERANCE

Liberal tolerance is grounded in *relativism*, the view that no one point of view on moral and religious knowledge is objectively correct for every person in every time and place. This notion, as understood and embraced in popular culture, feeds on the fact of *pluralism*, the reality of a plurality of different and contrary opinions on religious and moral matters. Against this backdrop, many in our culture conclude that one cannot say that one's view on religious and moral matters is better than anyone else's view. They assert that it is a mistake to claim that one's religious beliefs are exclusively correct and that believers in other faiths, no matter how sincere or devoted, hold false beliefs. Thus, *religious inclusivism* is the correct position to hold.

Relativism, pluralism, and religious inclusivism are the planks in a creed that does not tolerate any rivals. Its high-minded commitment to "openness" prohibits the possibility that anything is absolutely good, true, and beautiful. This was the central thesis of Alan Bloom's 1987 best seller, *The Closing of the American Mind*. Bloom writes: "The relativity of truth [for college students in American culture] is not a theoretical insight but a moral postulate, the condition of a free society, or so they see it.... The point is not to correct the mistakes and really be right; rather it is not to think you are right at all. The students, of course, cannot defend their opinion. It is something with which they have been indoctrinated...."[1]

According to Bloom, by dogmatically maintaining there is no truth, people who are relativists have become close-minded to the possibility of knowing the truth, if in fact it does exist. To understand what Bloom means, consider the following dialogue (based loosely on a real-life exchange) between a high school teacher and her student, Elizabeth:[2]

Teacher: Welcome, students. Since this is the first day of class, I want to lay down some ground rules. First, since no one has the truth, you should be open-minded to the opinions of your fellow students. Second....Elizabeth, do you have a question?

Elizabeth: Yes, I do. If nobody has the truth, isn't that a good reason for me not to listen to my fellow students? After all, if nobody has the truth, why should I waste my time listening to other people and their opinions. What would be the point? Only if somebody has the truth does it make sense to be open-minded. Don't you agree?

Teacher: No, I don't. Are you claiming to know the truth? Isn't that a bit arrogant and dogmatic?

Elizabeth: Not at all. Rather, I think it's dogmatic, as well as arrogant, to assert that there is not one person on earth who knows the truth. After all, have you met every person in the world and quizzed them exhaustively? If not, how can you make such a claim? Also, I believe it is actually the opposite of arrogance to say that I will alter my opinions to fit the truth whenever and wherever I find it. And if I happen to think that I have good reason to believe I do know the truth and would like to share it with you, why won't you listen to me? Why would you automatically discredit my opinion before it is even uttered? I thought we were supposed to listen to everyone's opinion.

Teacher: This should prove to be an interesting semester.

Another student: (blurts out): Ain't that the truth. (the students laugh)

The proponent of liberal tolerance, it turns out, is not the celebrant of diversity he portrays himself to be. Perhaps another example, one from popular culture, will be instructive. In 1997, in her acceptance speech for an Emmy for cowriting the "coming out" episode of *Ellen*, Ellen DeGeneres said, "I accept this on behalf of all people, and the teen-agers out there especially, who think there is something wrong with them because they are gay. There's nothing wrong with you. Don't ever let anybody make you feel ashamed of who you are."

There are many who, after hearing or reading Ellen's speech, applauded her for her liberal sensibilities, concluding that the actress is an open and tolerant person who is merely interested in helping young people better understand their own sexuality. If you think this way, you are mistaken. Ellen's speech is an example of what I call "passive-aggressive tyranny." The trick is to sound "passive" and accepting of "diversity" while at the same time putting forth an aggressively partisan agenda and implying that those who disagree are not only stupid but also harmful. In order to understand this point, imagine if a conservative Christian Emmy-award winner had said, "I accept this on behalf of all people, and the teen-agers out there especially, who think there is something wrong with them because they believe that human beings are made for a purpose and that purpose includes the building of community with its foundation being heterosexual monogamy. There's nothing wrong with you. Don't ever let anybody, especially television script writers, make you feel ashamed because of what you believe is true about reality." Clearly this would imply that those who affirm liberal views on sexuality are wrong. An award winner who made this speech would be denounced as narrow, bigoted, and intolerant. That person could expect never again to work in Hollywood.

Ironically, Ellen's Emmy speech does the same to those with

whom she disagrees. By encouraging people to believe there is nothing wrong with their homosexuality, she is saying there is something wrong with those (i.e., Christians and other social conservatives) who don't agree with this prescription. This condemnation is evident in the script of the show for which Ellen won an Emmy. In that famous "coming out" episode, the writers presumed that one is either bigoted or ignorant if one thinks Ellen's homosexuality is deviant and that such a one is incapable of having a thoughtful, carefully wrought case against homosexuality. Such hubris is astounding. It presumes not only that Ellen's detractors are wrong but also that they are stupid, irrational, and evil and should not even be allowed to make their case. They are, in a word, diseased, suffering from that made-up ailment, "homophobia."

What a strange way to attack one's opponents! After all, whether one fears homosexuals is irrelevant to the question of whether homosexual practice is natural, healthy, and moral. No one would say that the arguments of an antiwar protestor should not be taken seriously on the grounds that he is "hemophobic," that is, fearful of bloodshed. Moreover, if one is homophobic (assuming there is such a thing), that is, suffering from a phobia as one would suffer from claustrophobia, then the homophobe cannot help himself and is therefore suffering from a mental disorder, perhaps one that is the result of his genes. Consequently, calling someone homophobic is tantamount to making fun of the handicapped, unless of course the accuser is himself homophobic.

Ms. DeGeneres has every right to think those who don't agree with her judgments on human sexuality are wrong. The problem is that she and her more cerebral and sophisticated colleagues present their judgments as if they were not judgments. They believe their views to be in some sense "neutral." From their perspective they are merely letting people live any way they choose. But this is not neutral at all. It presupposes a particular and controversial view of human nature, human community, and human happiness. It assumes that only three elements, if present, make a sexual practice morally permissible: adult consent, one's desire, and the lack of intrusion into another person's lifestyle orientation (i.e., "it doesn't hurt anybody").

This, of course, is not obvious. For example, an adult male who receives gratification as a result of pedophile fantasies while secretly viewing his neighbor's young children, though he never acts on his fantasies and nobody ever finds out, is acting consistently with these three elements. Nevertheless, it seems counterintuitive to say what he is doing is on par with heterosexual monogamy and ought to be treated as such. By what principle can the Ellenites exclude this gentleman from the "tolerance" they accord more chic sexual orientations? At the end of the day, Ellen's viewpoint is one that affirms what its proponents believe is good, true, and beautiful, while implying that those who dispute this viewpoint are incorrect. Ellen is as intolerant and narrow as her detractors.

In the words of Lieutenant Columbo, the proponent of liberal tolerance is pulling a fast one. She eschews reason, objective morality, and exclusivity, while at the same time proposing that liberal tolerance is the most high-minded, righteous, and philosophically correct perspective that any reflective person with a university education can possibly embrace. Even the most sophisticated defenders of this viewpoint, whether intentionally or not, cannot seem to avoid this philosophical faux pas.

A MORE SOPHISTICATED DEFENSE

Consider the work of social scientists Jung Min Choi and John W. Murphy. They argue that although there are no objective universal norms of knowledge and morality, there are interpretive communities (i.e., cultures, civilizations, nations, ethnic heritages, etc.) within which objective norms are valid. Choi and Murphy explain: "Each community, accordingly, values certain norms. Therefore, some norms may be irrelevant in a specific community, because behavior is not random but is guided by expectations that are known by every competent member of a region. Exhibiting just any behavior would certainly result in a negative sanction. Within an interpretive community the idea that anything goes [i.e., relativism] is simply ridiculous, for all norms do not have equal validity."[3]

Supporters of this view deny it is relativistic because, they argue, it affirms that each community has its own "absolute" norms of knowledge and morality, though these norms do not apply to other communities. For example, if I live in community X and my community believes it is morally permissible to torture babies for fun and you live in community Y, which maintains that it is morally wrong to torture babies for fun, according to Choi and Murphy, there are no moral norms that transcend communities X and Y by which we can say that Y's opposition to torturing babies is better than X's acceptance of torturing babies.

Perhaps another example will help clarify this view. Suppose that the people in community X believe that the best method of making major medical decisions in life is consulting the zodiac and/or a Ouija Board. So, for example, if Dr. Jones recommends an appendectomy for Mr. Smith but the Ouija Board says no, then it would be best for Mr. Smith not to undergo the appendectomy. Now, the people in community Y used to believe the same thing as the people in X, but they have discovered through numerous double-blind experiments that consulting the zodiac and/or Ouija Board was no better than guessing, flipping a coin, or just plain luck. The people in Y rely on the science behind their medicine as a major part of their decision-making and for that reason have far fewer number of dead patients than community X.

If Choi and Murphy are correct that norms of knowledge are community-relative, then there is no basis for asserting that community Y's view of medical knowledge and decision-making is better than the view held by community X. Yet, it is clear that Y's perspective is more true, and for that reason results in a larger body of life-saving knowledge than X's perspective.

Even though they may deny it, the position defended by Choi and Murphy, and those who agree with their perspective, is relativism. It denies that there are universal norms of knowledge and morality that transcend diverse cultures and communities.

When Choi and Murphy attempt to marshal a philosophical defense of their viewpoint, their position unravels, for they are unable to defend their position without relying on the very notions they deny. For example, Choi and Murphy, after arguing for the concept of interpretive communities, go on to defend the work of literary scholar Stanley Fish, by arguing that

sociologists of various hues have verified a long time ago what Fish is saying. Symbolic interactionists, for example, have illustrated that persons evaluate their actions with regard to their respective "reference groups." Therefore, in terms of a single city, very different pockets of norms may be operative. To understand what deviance means in each circumstance, a priori definitions of normativeness must be set aside. For norms are embedded in symbols, signs, and gestures that may be very unique and restricted to a specific locale.

Upon crossing one of these relatively invisible boundaries, an individual quickly learns which behaviors are acceptable. This diversity, moreover, has not resulted in the disaster that conservatives predict. Yet navigating through this montage of norms requires interpretive skill, tolerance, and an appreciation for pluralism. *(94, emphases added)*

We learn from this quote that such sociologists *verify* the perspective that knowledge and morality are bound by interpretative communities. Apparently sociologists, at least the sociologists who verify this perspective, are not restricted by their interpretive communities. To claim that sociologists verify this perspective as true is to say that they *have knowledge* about reality. According to Choi and Murphy, however, this is impossible, for we are all (including sociologists) restricted by our interpretive communities. In other words, if these sociologists are restricted by their interpretive communities, and thus can give us no objective knowledge of reality, how can Choi and Murphy claim that their viewpoint has been "verified"? It seems, therefore, that Choi and Murphy must ironically presuppose that one can have knowledge of the real world in order to verify the perspective that one cannot have knowledge of the real world. But if their perspective is the correct one, the norms and observations put forth by these sociologists as well as Choi and Murphy cannot be true claims about the world. Thus, the appeal to sociologists who "verify" this view presupposes that the view itself is false!

In addition, Choi and Murphy presuppose certain objective moral norms when they maintain that interpretive skill, tolerance, and appreciation for pluralism are virtues by which one navigates "through this montage of norms," for this view is offering objective moral guidelines that apparently transcend any particular interpretive community. Put differently, Choi and Murphy are requiring that all people, regardless of what interpretive community in which they may reside, abide by certain universal objective moral norms. Yet, if this is not what they mean, then these virtues do not have to be followed by the members of some interpretive communities that don't accept these norms (e.g., Nazi Germany, a skin-head commune, or a group of sociopaths). Of course, it is absurd for any moral theory not to account for the objective wrong of Nazism, neo-Nazism, or the callous disregard for others.

Liberal Tolerance and the 2000 Southern Baptist Convention

In addition to what we have covered thus far, there are other ways by which we may defend the Christian worldview in a culture that celebrates liberal tolerance. Consider the recent controversy over the plans of the Southern Baptist Convention (SBC) to evangelize Jews, Muslims, and Hindus in the summer of 2000 in conjunction with its meeting in Chicago. SBC plans to bring 100,000 missionaries for the task. But this does not sit well with religious leaders who embrace liberal tolerance. According to a 28 November 1999 story in the

Chicago Tribune, "The Council of Religious Leaders of Metropolitan Chicago, representing the Catholic Archdiocese of Chicago and 39 other major Christian and Jewish institutions, sent a letter Saturday [27 Nov. 1999] warning that the high-profile evangelical blitz proposed by the Southern Baptists in June would poison interfaith relations and indirectly contribute to violence."[4]

The letter states that "while we are confident that your volunteers would come with entirely peaceful intentions, a campaign of the nature and scope you envision could contribute to a climate conducive to hate crimes."[5] Although the letter acknowledges the Baptists' constitutional right to religious expression, "it cites last July's [1999] shooting of six Jews in West Rogers Park and vandalism of a mosque in Villa Park in May as evidence of the vulnerability of people targeted because of their faith."[6] It is interesting to note that the Council did not tease out its own logic and conclude that perhaps its call for Southern Baptist self-censorship while connecting a time-honored Christian practice (i.e., evangelism) to vandalism and battery could itself "contribute to a climate conducive to hate crimes" and result in the Baptists themselves being victims.

In any event, how should we as Christians respond to such hysterical and outrageous assessments of our Christian practice? First, the Council is not claiming that Christian doctrine is false, but rather, it is claiming that religious beliefs are not legitimate claims to knowledge at all. So it is not that the Southern Baptists are mistaken about the truth of Christianity; they are mistaken about the nature of religion. For if the Council truly believed that religious doctrines, and Christian truth claims in particular, are claims to real knowledge, they would not have relied on demagoguery and scare tactics to make their point. In other words, the Southern Baptists are dangerous not because Christianity is false and they believe it is true, but because they really believe that Christianity is true and they believe other people from contrary religious traditions should become Christians as well. This, for the proponent of liberal tolerance, is absurd, because, as we have seen, liberal tolerance is grounded in relativism — the view that no one point of view on moral and religious knowledge is objectively correct for every person in every time and in every place.

This is why Bishop C. Joseph Sprague (of United Methodist Church's Northern Illinois Conference) can say of the Southern Baptists' plans for evangelism in Chicago: "I'm always fearful when we in the Christian community move beyond the rightful claim that Jesus is decisive for us, to the presupposition that non-Christians... are outside God's plan of salvation. That smacks of a kind of non-Jesus-like arrogance."[7] Of course, if Jesus' disciples had followed the Bishop's advice rather than their Lord's Great Commission, there would have been no Christianity as we know it today, if at all, and hence no Methodist bishops calling for the revocation of the Great Commission.

Second, the Council's letter is itself a form of evangelism for the gospel of liberal tolerance, for it is suggesting that the Southern Baptists, the letter's target, abandon their religious tradition and embrace the Council's relativist view of religious truth. If the Southern Baptists don't follow this suggestion, then there will be a type of punishment (i.e., "a campaign of the nature and scope you envision could contribute to a climate conducive to hate crimes"). Like most calls for openness and sensitivity by proponents of liberal tolerance, the Council's letter in reality calls for neither. It requires its recipient ei-

ther to behave and think in accordance with what the Council believes is the only appropriate way for religious believers to behave
and think or to be prepared to face opposition. This opposition may
include everything from uncharitable judgments (e.g., "non-Jesus-
like arrogance") to threats of violence (e.g., "could contribute to a climate conducive to hate crimes") to far-fetched McCarthyesque guilt
by association accusations (e.g., "last July's [1999] shooting of six
Jews in West Rogers Park and vandalism of a mosque in Villa Park
in May [cited] as evidence of the vulnerability of people targeted because of their faith").

The Tribune article states that the timing of the Council letter
"throws Chicago into the center of a debate already raging in other
parts of the nation."[8] A couple of examples are cited: "In New York, a
Jewish coalition protested a Southern Baptist campaign to pray for
the conversion of Jews during the Jewish High Holidays in September. A similar campaign Nov. 7 targeted Hindus on their holiday, Di-
wali, triggered protests not only across India but also outside a
Southern Baptist church in Boston."[9]

These examples are instructive because they show the incoherence of liberal tolerance. In neither case were the Southern Baptists
interfering with, or calling for the state or any other agency or group
to interfere with, the worship or religious practice of the Jews and
Hindus, for whose conversion they were praying. In fact, the Southern Baptists were exhibiting true tolerance. They showed respect for
the religious freedom of those who did not share their faith, while at
the same time praying for them to come to a belief in what the Southern Baptists believe is the truth. On the other hand, both the Jews
and the Hindus tried to exert public pressure on the Southern Bap-

tists through protest so that they would cease to engage in fundamental practices of their Christian faith, that is, prayer and evangelism. If anything, the Jews and Hindus showed less tolerance than the Southern Baptists, whom they sought to silence.

I do not doubt that some Hindus and Jews fail to appreciate and understand why Southern Baptists would choose their holidays to pray for their conversion, and that they find this practice offensive. But do these Hindus and Jews understand and appreciate that, because evangelism is a central aspect of the practice of Christian faith, when they tell Christians not to pray for them the Christians are equally offended?

Just as the Southern Baptists hope that non-Christians are converted to what Christians believe is true about God and religion, proponents of liberal tolerance hope that the Southern Baptists are converted to what proponents of liberal tolerance believe is true about God and religion, namely, relativism. Both groups are committed to a creed they will not compromise, though only the Southern Baptists seem thoughtful enough to understand this. The liberally tolerant are not as insightful, for they do not see their dogmas as dogmas. For that reason, in the name of liberty and tolerance they will likely continue to use their social and political power to punish Christians and others who will not submit to their doctrines.

THE SHAM OF LIBERAL TOLERANCE

Liberal tolerance is a sham. Although portrayed by its advocates as an open, tolerant, and neutral perspective, it is a dogma whose proponents tolerate no rivals. Those of us who are concerned with presenting and defending our faith in a post-Christian culture must be aware of this sort of challenge, one that masquerades as open, tolerant, and liberating, but in reality is dogmatic, partisan, and coercive.

Although the Christian worldview is marginalized in our culture and considered dangerous by some, we cannot lose our confidence. After all, this is God's universe, and He has made human beings in His image. We must be confident that when we unpack these undeniable notions that are "written on our hearts," those who unreflectively and unthinkingly dismiss our case really do know the truth as well (Rom. 2:15). But this must be balanced with the knowledge that the human heart is incredibly wicked (Jer. 17:9). This tension will remain as long as we attempt to defend our faith in a culture hostile to the God of Abraham, Isaac, Jacob, and Jesus of Nazareth.

Francis J. Beckwith is Professor of Philosophy and Church-Studies at Baylor University. In 2008-09 he is serving on the faculty of the University of Notre Dame as the Mary Ann Remick Senior Visiting Fellow in Notre Dame's Center for Ethics & Culture.

This article first appeared in the *Christian Research Journal,* volume 22, number 3 (2000).

---

1. Alan Bloom, *The Closing of the American Mind* (New York: Simon & Schuster, 1987), 25.
2. This dialogue originally appeared in Francis J. Beckwith and Gregory Koukl, *Relativism: Feet Firmly Planted in Mid-Air* (Grand Rapids: Baker, 1998), 74.
3. Jung Min Choi and John W. Murphy, *The Politics and Philosophy of Political Correctness* (Westport, CT: Praeger, 1992), 9394. The remaining citations of this book will appear in the text.
4. Steve Kloehn, Clergy Ask Baptists to Rethink Area Blitz, *The Chicago Tribune,* 28 November 1999, at www.chicagotribune.com/news/metro/chicago/

article/0,2669,ART-38638,FF.html (28 November 1999).
5. Council letter as quoted in ibid.
6. Kloehn.
7. Ibid.
8. Ibid.
9. Ibid.

VIEWPOINT
The Antiquity of Postmodernism

Postmodernism is supposedly the latest threat to the gospel of Jesus Christ and is being handled with a certain degree of trepidation, as if it is some new and strange phenomenon. It appears Christians have been caught off guard, for just as we were beginning to effectively address Modernism, it dissipated, leaving us in the structureless, ground-shifting, morass that is post-modern society.

Yet, even a cursory review of early church history will confirm that the central figure of the gospel was born into a cultural scene not unlike our own and, furthermore, the gospel spread rapidly in such an environment. For this reason, two points seem to follow:

1. Contrary to what the postmodernist prophets who populate our Western universities would have us believe, their latest and greatest philosophy is not "new" at all. This serves to reinforce Solomon's astute observation: "There is nothing new under the sun."[1]
2. The gospel is not at all threatened by this worn out philosophy dressed up in a new disguise, and therefore Christians should not feel at all intimidated in addressing it directly without apology.

The slippery nature of postmodernism makes it difficult to describe in simple terms. Os Guinness, Senior Fellow at Trinity Forum, offers a good working definition, "There is no truth, only truths. There are no principles, only preferences. There is no grand reason, only reasons. There is no privileged civilization (or culture, beliefs, periods, and styles), only a multiplicity of cultures, beliefs, periods, and styles. There is no universal justice, only interests and the competition of interest groups. There is no grand narrative of human progress, only countless stories of where people and their cultures are now. There is no simple reality or any grand objectivity of universal, detached knowledge, only a ceaseless representation of everything in terms of everything else."[2] Historian Gertrude Himmelfarb puts it in capsule form: "Postmodernism is the denial of the very idea of truth, reality, objectivity, reason or facts — all words which postmodernists now actually put in quotation marks! It's a totally permissive philosophy — anything goes — and it's extraordinary how far it has gone!"[3]

It is interesting that God became a man at a point in time and in a milieu very similar to the one in which we find ourselves. After all, He had a choice. He was born into a province of the mighty

Roman Empire. The place was teeming with Greeks, Romans, Jews, Africans, Syrians, and other Near Eastern peoples. It was a multicultural, pluralistic region rife with political turbulence and intrigue. There was a wide array of competing, and sometimes collaborating, interest groups. In addition to Judaism, polytheistic and pantheistic pagan religions proliferated. The occult of Babylonian roots was prevalent in many circles. Oriental and Egyptian mysticism were commonplace.

It is onto this unlikely scene that Christ appeared, boldly making the exclusive and rather "politically incorrect" statement that He is the Way, the Truth, and the Life.[4] Consider such a profound disclosure in the context in which it was presented. He knew the context. He knew the audience. He knew the power of what He was saying.

Later the apostles and early Christians lived and worked in a similar setting. Renowned biblical scholar, Dr. William Barclay, describes the first few centuries of Christian history as "an age when men accepted a kind of amalgam of religions. The Roman Emperor Alexander Severus had in his private chapel images of Abraham, Orpheus, Apollonius and Christ. Maximus of Tyre said that 'God is a name that all religions share.' Symmachus said in a speech in the Roman senate: 'There cannot be one way to so great a secret.' "[5] How did the apostles face such a seemingly daunting situation? They wrote and circulated letters like Colossians with its tremendous Christology. Jesus Christ is the image of the invisible God: in Him all the fullness of God is pleased to dwell. In Him are hidden all the treasures of wisdom and knowledge. In Him all the fullness of deity dwells in a body. Christ is all sufficient; nothing and no one else is needed.[6] In a syncretistic world the early Christians insisted on the unique

Christ. Through their word and daily conduct they held Christ and His work up for all to see, to compare, and to decide. They made claims and gave solid reasons for their claims.[7]

In this manner the gospel spread and was firmly believed by many from all walks of life. Young and old. Jew and Gentile. Male and female. Scholar and hedonist. Aristocrat and plebeian. Praetorian guard and foot soldier. What was the big attraction? The attraction was a unique Person in contrast to the meaningless banal fare of the day. Jesus and the apostles did not seek by coercion to eliminate the religions, cultures, and political groups that existed around them, nor were they intimidated by their existence. Let them compete in the cluttered marketplace of ideas. Bring all contenders and let's compare them to the Christ. Let's compare claims and reasons for claims. Let's compare a God of covenant with the whimsical gods of pagan mythologies. Let's compare the old covenant of the Jewish religion with the new covenant enacted by the blood of Christ. Which is better? Which is more efficacious?

Up until recently Christians in the Western world have lived a charmed life. We have been Christians presenting the gospel to quasi-Christians. Close to two thousand years of a Judeo-Christian culture has laid the foundational work for us. There are even some among us in evangelical circles who have adopted the role of historical revisionists and wax romantic about the "good old" medieval days when the so-called Church (read: cleric run Christianity) ruled society and there was only one religion, i.e., "Christian." Listening to them one would think their ideal for America is a modern version of medieval Europe. They neglect to point out the glaring difficulties with such nostalgia. Notably, pre-Renaissance was also pre-Reformation. For it was the Reformation that finally broke the stranglehold of the cleric class on society. The Reformation initiated the printing of the Bible and other books in the vernacular tongues for the non-classical Latin peoples to read for themselves if they were literate, or at least hear it being read in their own language.[8] The Renaissance and the Reformation were a justifiable reaction against a coercive and oppressive Christianity whose corrupt ruling class imposed its will on the people, keeping them in a collective state of superstitious ignorance and fear.

As an aside, it should be mentioned that those in secular academia who smugly attack Christianity are, for the most part, attacking the medieval "imperialistic" version of it, as if that version were a true representation of original Christian thought and practice as presented by Christ and the apostles. Whether this is done purposefully, or due to a profound ignorance, their young audiences leave the crowded lecture halls with a false impression of the Christian faith. It is completely understandable that they would reject such a false impression in favor of postmodernism or whatever the specific professor's pet philosophy happens to be at the time. However, in this blurry context, they are not rejecting the gospel at all or even a reasonable facsimile of it. It is imperative that we know the difference if we are effectively to help others make these distinctions. Let us be sure that if someone rejects the gospel it is indeed the *gospel* they are rejecting.

As we approach the closing of this millenium, the philosophy of postmodernism is upon us, and many Christians are running for cover as if the gospel isn't powerful enough to handle it. Some of us are nervously writhing our hands about living in a pluralistic society (which isn't going away any time soon), implying that the gospel isn't able to stand alone as an attractive and viable proposition without being propped up by a supportive pro-Christian cultural infrastructure. Those more assertive among us are attempting to address the issue by massaging the gospel in a good-hearted but feeble attempt at making it more palatable for the postmodern mind. This is of course a futile exercise, as there is no real way to effectively massage the gospel. It is what it is and has never changed. It is still "the power of God unto salvation."[9]

I submit, at the end of the day, that the postmodern mind needs to hear exactly what the minds of antiquity heard. The same startling question ringing through the ages: What think ye of Christ? — Paul Kerr

Paul Kerr is a scholar dedicated to providing thoughtful analysis and commentary to encourage the Christian community in tirelessly and effectively contending for the faith.

This article originally appeared in *Christian Research Journal*, volume 22, number 1 (1999).

---

1 Ecclesiastes 1:9
2 Os Guinness, *Fit Bodies Fat Minds* (Grand Rapids, MI: Baker Books, 1994), 105.
3 Quoted in Jo Ann Lewis, "It's Postmodern and If you Don't Get It You Don't Get It," *Washington Post* (March 27, 1995): G6.
4 John 14:6
5 William Barclay, *A Beginner's Guide to the New Testament*, (Louisville, KY: Westminster Knox Press, 1992), 58.

6   Colossians 1:15–20, 2:3, 9, 10
7   1 Corinthians 15:3–6
8   A treatise by Martin Luther titled, *On Christian Liberty* was one of these "other books." It was devoted to the proposition that by faith alone we are made righteous and through faith all believers are priests, i.e., the universality of the priesthood. In his book, *Great Turning Points in History*, Louis Snyder describes the impact of Luther's literary work, "Pope Leo X was at first disposed to treat Luther's defection lightly, but he soon realized that the pen of the German heretic was shaking the Church to its very foundations. On June 15, 1520, he sent Johann Maier of Eck to the Germanies with a papal bull of excommunication, in which Luther was called upon to recant or face the wrath of the highest power of Christendom" (New York: Barnes & Noble Books, 1996), 60. Luther was summoned to give an account of his position before the Diet of Worms. Luther's defense was poignant and brief, "Unless I am convicted of error by the testimony of Scripture (for I place no faith in the mere authority of the Pope, or of councils, which have often erred, and which have contradicted one another, recognizing, as I do, no other guide but the Bible, the Word of God), I cannot and will not retract, for we must never act contrary to our conscience." Of this event, Lord Acton wrote, "Luther at Worms is the most important and pregnant fact in our history, for there he defied all authority, Pope, council, and Emperor alike."
9   Romans 1:16

THE ANTIQUITY OF POSTMODERNISM

VIEWPOINT

The Doctrine Debate: Why Doctrine Matters More than Ever

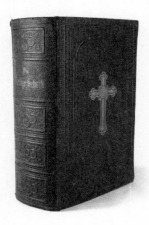

Doctrine is under attack.

Your initial response might be, "Of course it is, heretics have been challenging the foundations of the church since its inception!" and that is true, but today's attack not only targets particular doctrines held integral to true Christian faith (e.g. the Trinity, the incarnation, the existence of a literal hell, the inerrancy of Scripture), it also undermines the idea of doctrine itself, labeling it antiquated, irrelevant, and downright divisive. What's more, this assault on the heart of creedal Christianity is occurring not only from outside the church, but from inside as well.

In God's Word, it is true knowledge of Jesus Christ that brings transformation: "Then you will know the truth, and the truth will set you free" (John 8:32).[1] Eternal salvation depends not just upon believing in Christ, but also in believing accurately in Him: "For my Father's will is that everyone who looks to the Son and believes in him shall have eternal life…" (John 6:40). We recognize false prophets because they deny a key doctrine about Jesus, namely, that He came in the flesh (1 John 4:2). And Paul's encouragement to Titus is to appoint elders who will "hold firmly to the trustworthy message as it has been taught, so that he can encourage others by sound doctrine and refute those who oppose it" (Titus 1:9). Biblically and historically speaking, it is difficult to underestimate the importance of right doctrine.

Why Doctrine Matters. As a youth worker, I realize the necessity of helping young people to understand God and the Scriptures accurately. The reason is simple: *our view of God affects how we relate to God and others.* Wrong doctrine or the misrepresentation of right doctrine has consequences.

For instance, lacking a biblical perspective on heaven sets many young people up for discouragement and sin. In the minds of many youth heaven is like a dull, uninspiring church service. Most of them think there are certain pleasures they can experience only here on earth. Since God will forgive them, why not indulge now? Randy Alcorn says that some of Satan's favorite lies are about heaven, for Satan knows that if we truly understood the reality of heaven, it would radically transform our present lives.[2] We would have far more resolve and boldness if we understood and embraced the biblical doctrine of heaven.

The American missionary force has decreased substantially over the past fifty years. Albert Mohler believes the reason is that inclusivism and pluralism have seeped their way into the church: "At base, the issue is a failure of theological nerve—a devastating loss of biblical and doctrinal conviction...."[3] If salvation can be found apart from Christ, then why have a sense of urgency concerning the lost?

Given the importance of doctrine, it is distressing how biblically illiterate many Christians have become. In the "National Study of Youth and Religion" sociologist Christian Smith revealed that of conservative Protestant youth twenty-three percent are not sure of the existence of miracles, thirty-three percent maybe or definitely believe in reincarnation, and 41 percent disagree with the statement that people should practice only one faith. Smith concludes: "For a tradition that has so strongly emphasized infallibility or inerrancy of the Bible, the exclusive claims of conservative Christianity, and the need for a personal commitment of one's life to God, some of these numbers are astounding."[4] According to Smith, the church is at fault: "Our distinct impression is that very many religious congregations and communities of faith in the United States are failing rather badly in religiously engaging and educating their youth."[5]

Right Creeds, Right Deeds. Right doctrine should never be about just being right. Rather, the point of right doctrine is *always* about establishing and growing right relationships. Perfect doctrine without love is worthless. 1 Corinthians 13:2 says, "If I have the gift of prophecy and can fathom all mysteries and all knowledge, and if I have a faith that can move mountains, but have not love, I am nothing." Even the demons recognize good theology when they see it (James 2:19).

Orthodoxy (right belief) is meant to lead to orthopraxy (right practice). As my pastor puts it, "Right creeds lead to right deeds."

Paul regularly makes the necessary connection between doctrine and practice. For example, in his letter to the Ephesians he uses chapters one, two, and three to explain what God has accomplished through Jesus Christ. Then he spends the final three chapters (four, five, and six) to demonstrate how we should live in light of that truth. A similar pattern is found in both Colossians and Romans. There is one key difference in Romans: Paul spends eleven chapters on doctrine and five on application. The emphasis should be clear.

Though I do not agree with his philosophy of pragmatism, William James has practical insight important for the teaching of doctrine. He says for any idea we should always ask, "What difference does it make?" If it makes no existential difference to the way we live whether it is true or false, then according to James, we should not bother with it. When teaching doctrine we should be regularly asking, "So what?" How does belief in the Trinity affect my relationship to God and to others? How does belief in the sovereignty of God influence my view of the future? How does the incarnation affect my self-image? Much of the problem today is not with doctrine *per se*, but with our failure to connect doctrine to real life.

The Doctrine Difference. Numerous national studies conducted by pollsters such as The Gallup Organization, the Barna Group, and the Josh McDowell Ministry have revealed that the lives of Christians are largely indistinguishable from non-Christians. When it comes to divorce, materialism, and cohabitation, Christians differ only slightly from non-Christians (if at all). Fortunately, this is not the entire story.

George Barna makes a distinction between "born-again Christians without a biblical worldview" and "born-again Christians with a biblical worldview." Those without a biblical worldview have made a personal commitment to Jesus that is important to their lives and believe they will go to heaven because they have confessed their sins and accepted Jesus as Savior.

The criterion for Christians with a biblical worldview, on the other hand, is much more stringent. In addition to the aforementioned beliefs, they also hold that the Bible is the moral standard of absolute truth that is completely accurate in all its teachings and that God is the all-knowing, all-powerful Creator who still rules the universe. Barna has found that only nine percent of born-again adults and two percent of born-again youth have a biblical worldview.[6]

For those who question the importance of doctrine, it may come as a surprise that Christians with a biblical worldview live radically different than the world. Forty-nine percent volunteered more than an hour to an organization serving the poor, whereas only twenty-nine percent of born-again Christians *without* a biblical worldview and twenty-two percent of non-born-again Christians have done so. They are nine times more likely than all others to avoid "adult only" material on the Internet. They are twice as likely not to watch a movie specifically because it contained objectionable material and four times as likely to boycott objectionable products and companies.[7]

In *The Scandal of the Evangelical Conscience*, Ron Sider relates the importance of these findings to correct doctrine: "Barna's findings on the different behavior of Christians with a biblical worldview underline the importance of theology. Biblical orthodoxy does matter. One important way to end the scandal of contemporary Christian behavior is to work and pray fervently for the growth of orthodox theological belief in our churches."[8]

Isn't Doctrine Divisive? In previous articles for the CHRISTIAN RESEARCH JOURNAL, Norman Geisler distinguished between essential and nonessential doctrines of the Christian faith.[9] In terms of making salvation possible, essential doctrines include: (1) human depravity, (2) Christ's virgin birth, (3) Christ's sinlessness, (4) Christ's deity, (5) Christ's humanity, (6) God's unity, (7) God's triunity, (8) the necessity of God's grace, (9) the necessity of faith, (10) Christ's atoning death, (11) Christ's bodily resurrection, (12) Christ's bodily ascension, (13) Christ's present high priestly service, (14) Christ's second coming, final judgment (heaven and hell), and reign. Geisler makes three critical observations relevant to our discussion. First, the essential doctrines are the foundation for our unity. Second, the essential doctrines distinguish true Christianity from cultic spin-offs. Third, the only truths Christians should divide over are essential doctrines. The third point is most important for our purposes: the essential doctrines are nonnegotiable for followers of Christ and are matters over which we *should* divide.

There is a trend in the church today to elevate unity above truth. Many are willing to set aside essential doctrines for the sake of harmony. While unity is a prime virtue for the body of Christ, it should not come at the expense of truth. In the Sermon on the Mount, Jesus did emphasize the importance of peacemaking, but he was not afraid to criticize false teaching—calling his followers to "watch out for false prophets. They come to you in sheep's clothing, but inwardly they are ferocious wolves" (Matt. 7:15). Jesus saw the value in dividing over essential doctrine because it saves people from the consequences of false teaching.

It is ironic that some churches today have divided over the matter of whether churches should divide over doctrine! With further irony, the claim that Christians should *not* divide over doctrine is itself a doctrine. There is no way for a community to avoid having doctrinal beliefs. Community requires a shared set of ideas taken as authoritative. Even those who claim that doctrine should not be emphasized have their own authority claims that rule their particular communities.

True unity comes not when we sacrifice sound doctrine, but when we focus on the core truths of the gospel. Thus, the real question is not *if* we teach doctrine but *what* doctrines do we teach, *how* do we teach them, and do we live them out in relationships. For the sake of our youth and the vitality of the church, we must not cave into the pressure to stop teaching doctrine. The proper response to the attack on doctrine is not retreat, but to march forward with even greater resolve, unity, and love.—*Sean McDowell*

Sean McDowell graduated summa cum laude from Talbot Theological Seminary with a double Master's degree in Philosophy and Theology. He teaches Bible at Capistrano Valley Christian Schools in San Juan Capistrano, California, is a nationally recognized speaker, and has authored many articles and books.

This article originally appeared in *Christian Research Journal*, volume 31, number 1 (2008).

1   All Scripture quotations are from the *New International Version* (NIV).
2   Randy Alcorn, *Heaven* (Carol Stream, IL: Tyndale, 2004), 10–12.
3   Albert Mohler, "Missions at Risk—A Failure of Nerve" (www.crosswalk.com/ 1353434/, accessed on August 25, 2007).
4   Christian Smith and Melinda Lundquist Denton, *Soul Searching: The Religious and Spiritual Lives of American Teenagers* (New York: Oxford, 2005), 4344.
5   Smith and Denton, 262.
6   George Barna, *Think Like Jesus* (Brentwood, TN: Integrity Publishers, 2003), 23.
7   Ibid, 28–29.
8   Ronald J. Sider, *The Scandal of the Evangelical Conscience* (Grand Rapids: Baker Books, 2005), 129–130.
9   Norman L. Geisler, "The Essential Doctrines of the Christian Faith: A Historical Approach," *Christian Research* Journal, 28, 5 {2005), and Norman L. Geisler, "The Essential Doctrines of the Christian Faith: A Logical Approach," *Christian Research Journal*, 28, 6 (2005).

AFTERWARD
Standing Our Ground

*Most Christians would rather die than think—
in fact they do. —Bertrand Russell*

It will come as no surprise to even semi-alert observers that truth as we have known it is under siege. Assailed on multiple fronts by a seemingly endless barrage of "isms"—postmodernism, relativism, experientialism, hedonism, and philosophical naturalism to name a few—to many Christians truth has apparently become less and less defensible. Either because they perceive that truth has become so deconstructed, relativized, subjectivized, and otherwise vaporized that like Humpty Dumpty they don't know if it can be put back together again, or they believe (perhaps tacitly more than rationally) that objective truth exists but they are simply bewildered and befuddled as to how to defend their convictions and instincts.

That's where CRI and the CHRISTIAN RESEARCH JOURNAL come in. And where serious Christians like you can make a difference. How? By knowing where we stand. By standing our ground. And by standing together.

Epistemology

Understandably, the average Christian wouldn't know what epistemology is. And the truth be known, most Christians are much more interested in the *acts* of Jesus than exegesis. Most are quite content to leave epistemological, hermeneutical, and exegetical pursuits of truth to the rarified realms of academia.

But as serious thinkers know, *how* we know what we know is no small matter, and that means knowing *where* we stand. When we think of standing our ground, the terms "standing" and "ground" are significant for epistemological as well as existential reasons, because *episteme* is the thing on which we stand (*epi* means 'upon,' and *[hi]stanai* means 'to stand'). Thus, epistemology implies the act of standing as well as the ground on which one stands.

Where does the Christian stand? Not on the perennially shifting sands of cultural and intellectual fashion nor on the porous platitudes of politically correct secularists whose only god is tolerance. Instead, the Christian stands on the unshakable rock of revelation, God's Word tested through the ages. Both epistemologically as well as existentially, the greatest Christian scholars as well as the greatest saints have known the wisdom expressed by Alfred Lord Tennyson when he wrote, "Cast all your cares on God; that anchor holds."

Righteous Resistance

C. S. Lewis once wrote, "Enemy occupied territory. That is what the world is. And Christianity is the story of how the rightful king has landed in disguise and is calling us all to take part in a great campaign of sabotage." How radically different the tone of this battle cry than a definition of a conservative that was recently heard in our U.S. elections: "A conservative is one who sits and thinks, but mainly sits."

What all Christians must grasp, while truth is under siege, is that God has not called us to *sit* for the truth. He has called us to *stand* for the truth:

Put on the full armor of God, so that when the day of evil comes, you may be able to stand your ground, and after you have done every-thing, to stand. Stand firm then, with the belt of truth buckled around your waist, with the breastplate of righteousness in place, and with your feet fitted with the readiness that comes from the gospel of peace. In addition to all this, take up the shield of faith, with which you can extinguish all the flaming arrows of the evil one.

—Ephesians 6:13–16, NIV

For those Christians who inevitably feel the pressure of today's totalitarian tolerance and the implicit demand for impartiality when it comes to truth, consider the words of G. K. Chesterton: "Impar-tiality is a pompous name for indifference, which is an elegant name for ignorance."

Let's make no mistake. With truth under siege, this isn't a time for impartiality, indifference, or ignorance. And certainly not a time for timidity or cowardice. It is instead a time for righteous revolution-aries (or "sanctified saboteurs," as we recall the words of C. S. Lewis) who are willing to stand their ground because they have witnessed the deadly consequences when godless ideologies are not halted in their tracks. The twentieth century alone witnessed the deaths of tens of millions of people through Hitler's "Final Solution," Stalin's bestial genocide, and Mao's ruthless purges, revealing with painful clarity that when truth dies, countless millions of lives are often con-sumed in the wake.

Standing Together

We must all hang together, or assuredly we shall all hang separately. —Benjamin Franklin at the signing of the Declaration of Independence

As more and more of Western civilization moves precariously toward the brink of incoherence due to the slow death of objective truth, it is clear that we must not only know where we stand and stand our ground, but we must stand together. For JOURNAL readers and other alert Christian friends, this means we must *recognize* the assaults on truth before we can *resist* them.

Having recognized that truth is under siege, and that heresy advances only as orthodoxy retreats, what are our options? While the list of all that we could do would no doubt be lengthy, here are four steps each Christian can take:

First, study. Or by way of elaboration, "Do your best to present yourself to God as one approved, a workman who does not need to be ashamed and who correctly handles the word of truth" (2 Timothy 2:15). This means getting into the Word of God so that the Word of God can get into you. The acronym MEALS is helpful here:

Memorize—Make Scripture *memorization* a lifestyle. Knowing portions of the Bible helps you meditate on them.

Examine—Use your mind to honor God and *examine* the teachings of men in the light of Scripture.

Apply—Take the knowledge you glean from the Word of God and *apply* it to every aspect of your daily life.

Listen—*Listen* carefully as God speaks to you through the mystery
of His Word.
Study—*Study* so that you might handle the Word of God correctly.

Make a commitment to yourself and to the Lord that while others
may *sit* on the truth, *you will stand.* (And please harbor no doubts
as to whether God can use you where you are. He certainly can't use
you where you're not!)

Second, pray. As Martin Tupper, the nineteenth-century English
writer and poet aptly put it, "Prayer is the slender nerve that moves
the muscle of Omnipotence." To attempt to stand against today's assaults on truth without the power of prayer is sheer folly. Ask those
who have tried to "gut it out" on their own power. As strategy or tac-
tic, it's a losing battle. Rather than a neutral and dispassionate exchange of ideas, this is spiritual warfare and a bloody battle for
perspectives on reality!

Third, consider standing together with CRI. Whether it's
through the JOURNAL, the *Bible Answer Man* broadcast, or the increasingly diverse, far-reaching, and potent media channels in CRI's
arsenal for truth, we're laboring to help you—and Christians every-
where—to be equipped to stand for Truth. Not timidly and reluc-
tantly, but *boldly* and *confidently.* That means being able, with
passionate conviction and laser clarity, to answer the questions and
withstand the challenges that are increasingly being posed to ill-pre-
pared Christians. If you're not already a member of CRI's support
team, visit our Web site at www.equip.org to make a gift today (or

see the several ways of contacting CRI listed at the back of this book). Or better yet, become a member of our monthly support team, a member of our CRI Fellowship, or even our President's Council.

Fourth, introduce a friend, family member, or associate to CRI. Whether it's listening to the *Bible Answer Man* broadcast, subscribing to the Journal, purchasing life-changing resources from our online e-store, or supporting CRI's work financially or with prayer, every "enlistment" in the army for truth helps to shift the tide of the battle. And remember the profound words of Abraham Kuyper:

When principles that run against your deepest convictions begin to win the day, then battle is your calling, and peace has become sin; you must, at the price of dearest peace, lay your convictions bare before friend and enemy, with all the fire of your faith.

—*Hank Hanegraaff*

WHAT IS TRUTH?
Study Questions

"What is Truth?" by Hank Hanegraaff

The idea that Christianity is true because it works is *pragmatism*. In reality, however, believers live out their faith in Christ in deep and practical ways *because* Christianity is true. Moreover, Christianity is true even in situations where being a Christian seems impractical or inconvenient. In countries where Christians are persecuted (e.g., China), it may not be practical or convenient to profess faith in Christ, for that might mean prison or worse, and yet that does not mean the Christian message is untrue. Suppose someone were to ask, "The Bible may have had practical application for people who lived 2,000 years ago in a desert, but wouldn't it be better for free-thinking people today to determine what works for them without consulting a supposed 'Holy Book'?" How would you respond?

Some people hold to an idea or religious belief simply because it feels good. It is their *subjective experience* alone that tells them what is true and what is false. What is wrong with that kind of thinking?

Relativism is the idea that what is true (or right) for you is not necessarily true (or right) for me. Consider the following two statements: 1) All Christians are truth–tellers; 2) Not all Christians are truth–tellers. Can both statements be true in the same way at the same time? Why or why not?

Living forthrightly and consistently in light of truth is no easy task. Consider the apostle Peter. At one point he boldly confessed that Jesus is the Christ, the Son of the living God, and declared that he would go to his death for the sake of the Lord (Matt. 16:16–22). Then he publicly denied his Lord three times (Matt. 26:69–74). Later, he preached the boldest of sermons on Pentecost (Acts 2). Yet, even as a Spirit-filled apostle, he again fell into hypocrisy by separating from Gentiles for fear of his fellow Jewish believers (Gal 2:11ff.). Historical tradition, finally, tells us that Peter did bravely die for his faith in Christ (see Eusebius, *Ecclesiastical History* 2:25). Consider almost every other hero of the Faith as recorded in Scripture, and similar inconsistencies appear between profession of faith and outward speech or action. What reasons (rationalizations) might we have for not living or speaking in accordance with truth at home, school, church, or work?

Hank Hanegraaff writes, "The death of truth spells the death of civilization." Try to explain why truth is vital to civilization.

"The Postmodern Challenge: Facing the Spirit of the Age" by Jim Leffel and Dennis McCallum

John wants to join the local Zen center for self-discipline. Mary likes the way Wicca empowers women. Bill sees all religious folks as a bunch of hypocrites, so he claims Satanism. Ed wants to become a Latter-day Saints missionary, because he read the *Book of Mormon* and felt the "burning in the bosom." Postmodernism is comfortable in accepting that they all have their faith story, and one should let them do what works for them, since there is no one dominating story [meta-narrative] out there. How would you respond to a person who shared that it was okay for everyone to have their own story? Would sharing with each of them about your belief in Jesus Christ be intolerant? Why or why not?

A church leader shares in a Bible study, "People today are not interested in hearing the evidence for Christianity. We are just going to confuse them by loading them with a bunch of truth-claims and theological words they can't understand. We just need to be more relational and loving." What is wrong with this thinking?

"That's your truth, not mine!" says the postmodernist. "The only reason you believe in Christianity is because you live in the United States. If you'd have grown up somewhere else, like Timbuktu, you'd have a totally different religion. The only objective truth is that there is no objective truth. Truth is relative and subjective!" Can something be objectively true whether or not any individual or culture believes it to be true? Why or why not?

Form a prayer list of names of people you know that have adopted postmodern thinking. What are some creative ways that you can use to help them understand the serious problems that their beliefs can have on their personal lives and society?

Think about the following statement and try to explain why you agree or disagree with it: The only reason one ought to believe anything is because it is true.

"Deconstructing Liberal Tolerance"
by Francis Beckwith

Recall the illustration of the school teacher who said, "Since no one has the truth, you should be open-minded to the opinions of your fellow students." What is wrong with her reasoning? In what ways would this kind of thinking prevent us from knowing what is good, true, and beautiful?

STUDY QUESTIONS

It is common to come across examples of liberal tolerance in TV, newspapers, magazines, books, art, music, etc. One example is the famous 1997 episode of *Ellen*, where the main character, Ellen DeGeneres, "comes out of the closet" or shares openly in public that she is gay, which won the sitcom an Emmy. In her acceptance speech, DeGeneres said, "I accept this on behalf of all people and the teenagers out there especially who think there is something wrong with them because they are gay. There's nothing wrong with you. Don't ever let anybody make you feel ashamed of who you are." Explain how DeGeneres's statement is actually an example of intolerance.

Gene Robinson, an openly gay Episcopalian bishop, in an interview on the BBC stated, "I do believe that the rhetoric of those who would gladly decide themselves as anti-gay certainly create an atmosphere in which a person who might contemplate violence would feel more justified."[1] Biblical Christianity condemns homosexuality. It also condemns unwarranted acts of violence against another person, such as gay *bashing*. Still, many Christians today who simply say, "Homosexuality is a sin," run the risk of being labeled by the "tolerant" as homophobic or someone who has an irrational fear of homosexuals. What can a Christian say in response to this?

Think of other current examples of liberal tolerance.

Christ calls all Christians to preach the gospel to the world; however, those who want to put their faith into action might well be criticized as "intolerant," "arrogant," and "indirectly contributing to hate crimes" against oppressed minorities. Explain the thinking behind these objections and point out the errors in such reasoning.

"The Antiquity of Postmodernism" by Paul Kerr

Why is postmodernism so hard to define?

In what ways is our present postmodern society similar to the society of Christ's time?

Reflect on Kerr's thesis that significant aspects of postmodern thinking are not new but actually ancient. Does this surprise you?

How is the "imperialistic" version of Christianity that is attacked by the postmodernist a caricature?

Moby, a popular music artist, blogged,

When i call myself a christian it's because i find christ's character and teachings to be incredibly compelling and, well, divine (cos they're too weird/impractical/perfect to have ever been invented by a human being). all of the other stuff: virgin birth, apocryphal gospels, did christ have a wife/brother/twin/dog/etc?, i find to be interesting window dressing. if someone came to me and said: 'i have proof that there was no virgin birth and that christ had a brother and a wife and a boston terrier!' i'd say: 'ok. but his teachings are still pretty remarkable, regardless of the circumstances of his life, right?' i also have great respect for other religions, especially those that stress the virtues of love and compassion and forgiveness and humility. and i'll never, not for a second, say, 'what i believe is right, and what you believe is wrong.' what i believe is what i believe. it's subjective and it makes sense to me and it changes as i change and as my experience in the world changes. constancy is not, in my opinion, defined through rigidity, but rather through love and adherence even through changing circumstances.[2]

This illustrates what Kerr refers to as "massaging the gospel in a good-hearted but feeble attempt at making it more palatable for the postmodern mind." If someone were to share such thoughts in a small group setting at your church, what might you say to address the assertions?

"The Doctrine Debate: Why Doctrine Matters More Than Ever" by Sean McDowell

Suppose that a member of your church connection group says that she is not interested in studying doctrine because such study has no "relevance." How would you explain to your friend the benefits of studying Christian doctrine?

What is a potential problem with adopting the wrong doctrines or misrepresentation of doctrines?

Explain how discussion about right doctrine is not just about winning an argument.

Another objection to studying doctrine is that it divides the church by separating Christians into factions committed to a doctrinal idea. Why is such avoidance of grappling with sound doctrine an unbiblical and dangerous way of trying to preserve Christian unity and community?

In light of the entire collection of essays in this book, what does it mean to claim that biblical doctrine is true, and how would you defend the claim that what the Bible teaches is true?

---

1 BBC, *Hardtalk*, April 30, 2008.
2 Moby.com, "I think it's odd/funny when people come to moby.com or

myspace to tell me about Christianity, " December 21, 2006, http://
www.moby.com/journal/2006-12-21/i_think_its_odd_funny_when_people_
come_m.html, last accessed March 9, 2009.

CHRISTIAN RESEARCH INSTITUTE

On the Internet (including 24-Hour Credit Card Ordering): www.equip.org

---

By Mail:
CRI United States
P.O. Box 8500
Charlotte, NC 28271-8500

In Canada:
CRI Canada
56051 Airways P.O.
Calgary, Alberta T2E 8K5

By Phone:
U.S. Toll-Free Customer Service Line
(888) 7000-CRI
Fax (704) 887-8299

Canada Toll-Free Credit Card Line
(800) 665-5851
Canada Customer Service
(403) 571-6363

On the Broadcast:
To contact the *Bible Answer Man* broadcast with your questions, call toll free in the U.S. and Canada, (888) ASK HANK (275-4265), Monday–Friday, 5:50 p.m. to 7:00 p.m. Eastern Time. For a list of stations airing the *Bible Answer Man* broadcast, or to listen online, log on to www.equip.org.